SCIENCE CORNER

Rocks and Soil

Alice Harman

Explore the world with **Popcorn -** your complete first non-fiction library.

Look out for more titles in the Popcorn range. All books have the same format of simple text and striking images. Text is carefully matched to the pictures to help readers to identify and understand key vocabulary.
www.waylandbooks.co.uk/popcorn

Published in paperback in 2014 by Wayland
Copyright © Wayland 2014

Wayland
Hachette Children's Books
338 Euston Road
London NW1 3BH

Wayland Australia
Level 17/207 Kent Street
Sydney NSW 2000

Produced for Wayland by
White-Thomson Publishing Ltd
www.wtpub.co.uk
+44 (0)843 208 7460

Editor: Alice Harman
Designer: Clare Nicholas
Picture researcher: Alice Harman
Series consultant: Kate Ruttle
Design concept: Paul Cherrill

British Library Cataloguing in Publication Data
Harman, Alice.
    Rocks and soil. -- (Science corner)(Popcorn)
    1. Rocks--Juvenile literature. 2. Soils--Juvenile
    literature.
    I. Title II. Series
    552-dc23

ISBN: 978 0 7502 8316 8

Wayland is a division of Hachette Children's Books,
an Hachette UK company.
www.hachette.co.uk

Printed and bound in China

10 9 8 7 6 5 4 3 2 1

Picture/illustration credits:
Peter Bull: 23; Stefan Chabluk: 18; Science Photo
Library: Sheila Terry 16t; Shutterstock: Scott Prokop
cover, oksana.perkins 4, Fotokostic 5, xfox01 5 (inset),
Mopic 6, Mariusz Niedwiedzki 7, Catmando 8, Tyler
Boyes (inset), dexns 9, Marcio Jose Bastos Silva 9
(inset), Anna Jurkovska 10, Dmitrijs Bindemanis 11,
Givaga 12, Filipe B. Varela, KOO 15, D. Kucharski &
K. Kucharska 15 (inset), Boyan Dimitrov 16b, Peter
Wollinga 17, topal 19, Matt Gibson 20, Dirk Ercken 21;
Wikimedia: 11 (inset), 12 (inset), 13.

Every effort has been made to clear copyright.
Should there be any inadvertent omission,
please apply to the publisher for rectification.

Contents

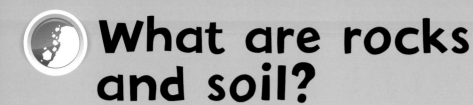

What are rocks and soil?

Rocks can be hard or soft, big or small, heavy or light. They come in lots of different colours and patterns. The surface of the Earth is made of rock.

Sandstone is a soft rock. It is worn down by wind and rain into amazing shapes.

Soil is made from small pieces of broken rock, dead leaves and other natural materials. It also contains water and air.

Most plants grow in soil. We need soil to grow food for ourselves and farm animals.

Inside the Earth

Most of the Earth is made of rock.
The surface of the Earth is called the
crust. The very hot, partly liquid rock
underneath is called the mantle.

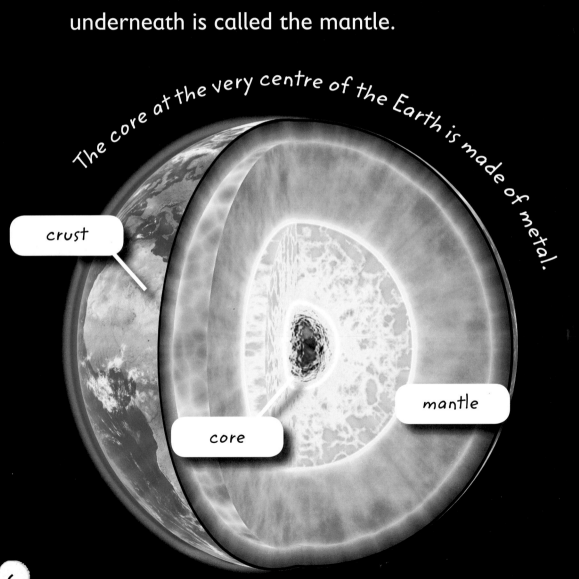

The core at the very centre of the Earth is made of metal.

crust

mantle

core

The crust is made of huge plates of rock. These plates move very slowly. When they push against each other, they form mountains.

High, rough mountains like these ones become lower and smoother over thousands of years.

7

Igneous and sedimentary rocks

Igneous rocks are made of hot liquid
rock that has cooled and hardened.
Liquid rock comes up onto the
Earth's surface through volcanoes.

A volcano is a hill built up around a hole in the Earth's crust.

Obsidian is an
igneous rock.

Sedimentary rocks are made of tiny pieces of rock, and sometimes shell and bone. Over time, these pieces are pressed together into layers of solid rock.

Dead plants and animals are often trapped in the rock. They are called fossils.

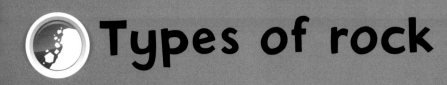

Types of rock

Some rocks, such as granite,
are very hard and strong.
Others, such as chalk, are
very soft and easily crumble.

We can write with chalk because it wears away when pressed against a hard surface.

Some rocks have tiny holes
that water can flow through.
Other rocks, such as slate,
do not let in any water.

People make roof tiles out of slate
because it keeps the house underneath dry.

Rocks and minerals

Rocks are made of small pieces of mineral. Some rocks are made of just one or two minerals. Other rocks contain lots of different minerals.

Granite is an igneous rock that is mostly made of a common mineral called quartz.

Some minerals, such as diamond, are very rare and expensive. People break apart the rock to look for these minerals.

There are more than 4,500 different types of minerals on Earth.

This very large diamond is still attached to the rock.

Life in the soil

Soil is full of nutrients that help plants grow. Plants have roots that take up water and nutrients from the soil. They need these things to stay alive.

As the plant grows above ground, its roots grow underground.

Earthworms eat dead leaves and other plant parts in the soil. They then poo in the soil. Their poo contains lots of nutrients that help plants to grow well.

Moles like to eat earthworms. These animals also live in the soil.

Types of soil

Soil contains three types of broken rock pieces. The smallest pieces are clay, the largest pieces are sand and the middle-sized ones are silt.

Soil with lots of clay is smooth. It can be very thick and heavy.

← Sandy soil is rough and mostly dry.

Different areas of land have soil with different amounts of clay, silt and sand. Some plants like to grow in dry, sandy soil and others grow best in clay soil.

Silt soil is very rich in nutrients, so many plants grow well in it.

The soil around the Amazon River contains lots of silt.

Soil layers

There are different layers of soil. The top layers contain the most plant and animal life, water and nutrients. The soil in the lower layers contains larger rocks.

Underneath the soil is the rocky crust of the Earth. This is also called bedrock.

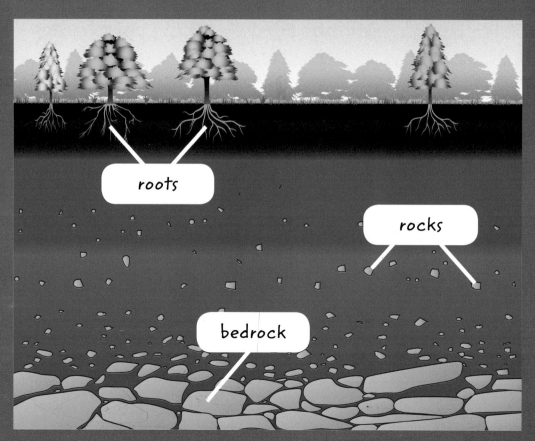

roots

rocks

bedrock

New layers of soil build up over time. Tiny pieces of big rocks slowly break off, and mix with dead plants and other materials to become soil.

People dig underground to find objects from the past that are covered by layers of new soil.

In dry places, soil becomes packed together. This makes it difficult to dig through.

19

Rock and soil erosion

Wind and water can slowly break tiny pieces off softer types of rock. This is called rock erosion.

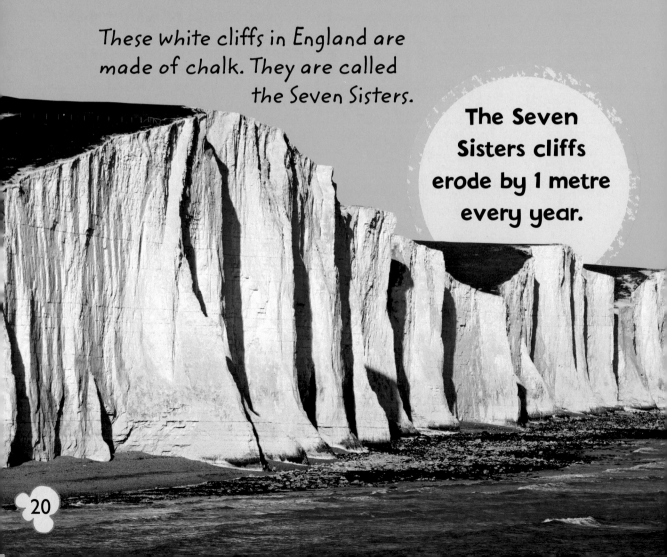

These white cliffs in England are made of chalk. They are called the Seven Sisters.

The Seven Sisters cliffs erode by 1 metre every year.

Wind and water erode soil. Plant roots help to hold the soil together. Without these plants, too much soil can blow or wash away.

Farm animals ate all the grass in this area. Plants cannot grow well now because of the soil erosion.

What am I?

Each of the sentences below describes something that you have learned about in this book. Try to work out which of the words listed here is the subject of each sentence.

a. fossil   b. rock   c. earthworm

d. clay   e. crust   f. mantle

1. I'm the layer of hard rock around the outside of the Earth.

2. I'm a solid material made of small pieces of mineral.

3. I'm the remains of a dead animal or plant trapped in the rock for many, many years.

4. I'm the hot, partly liquid rock under the surface of the Earth.

5. I'm a creature that lives in the soil, and my poo makes the soil better for plants that grow in it.

6. I'm the smallest type of broken rock piece found in the soil.

Answers: 1e. crust 2b. rock 3a. fossil 4f. mantle 5c. earthworm 6d. clay

Chocolate igneous rocks

You will need:
• saucepan • glass bowl
• a big chocolate bar, broken into pieces, or a big bag of chocolate chips
• wooden spoon • baking tray
• baking paper
• oven glove

1. Ask an adult to help you melt broken pieces of chocolate, or chocolate chips, in a bowl over a saucepan of hot water. This is how the rocks underneath the Earth's surface melt in high temperatures.

2. Help an adult to pour the melted chocolate onto a baking tray lined with baking paper. This is the movement of hot, liquid rock into a cooler place closer to the Earth's surface or above ground.

3. See what happens as the chocolate cools. It slowly hardens into a big piece of solid chocolate. This is what happens when liquid rock cools to form igneous rock.

4. Wait for the chocolate to cool completely, break it into pieces and then eat some!

Glossary

bone hard material that forms the skeleton of an animal

core centre of the Earth; it is made of very hard, hot metal

crumble fall apart easily into small pieces

liquid not solid or gas, and flows easily; water is a liquid

mineral material formed in the Earth that isn't an animal or a plant

nutrients things in food that help animals (including humans) and plants live and grow

pattern arrangement of repeated shapes, lines or colours

plates large pieces of the Earth's crust; they move very slowly on top of the liquid rock below

roots part of a plant that most often grows underground; they hold the plant in the soil, and take up water and nutrients

shell hard outer part of animals such as snails and crabs

surface top layer of something

tiles flat piece of hard material, such as rock; they are used to cover floors, walls and roofs

Index